MEDITERRANEAN BOWLS

COOKBOOK

80 Recipes for Healthy Greek, Spanish, Lebanese and Italian Bowls

Emma Yang

The trademarks that are used are without any consent, and the publication of the trademark is without permission or backing by the trademark owner. All trademarks and brands within this book are for clarifying purposes only and are the owned by the owners themselves, not affiliated with this document.

Contents

Introduction

Mediterranean food is popular since it is one of the healthiest on the globe. Because Mediterranean meals are prepared with fresh ingredients, the benefits of these recipes make them even more delectable. The diet emphasizes fresh foods such as berries, grains, herbs, veggies, and nuts.

Mediterranean cuisine refers to a variety of eating habits used by a wide range of people. It has nothing to do with a particular ethnic group or community. A variety of cultural factors influences Mediterranean cooking.
The world's earliest civilizations were founded on the Mediterranean Sea. Food land was enhanced by excellent soil and a moderate climate. Merchants who sold cultural goods like spice and other delicacies were drawn to their location at the crossroads of Europe, Asia, and Africa.

Colonization was another factor that impacted Mediterranean cuisine. The different cultures of the Mediterranean came into greater contact due to numerous civilizations' efforts to create empires.
In Mediterranean cuisine, olive oil is one of the most frequently utilized components. The region is densely forested with olive trees. Olives are an important ingredient in a variety of cuisines. Veggies are also essential. Zucchini, green beans, carrots, tomatoes, nuts and seeds, mushrooms, garlic, okra, eggplants, and a variety of greens and courgettes are also common vegetables. Meat is seldom consumed.

Because the Mediterranean's rough terrain does not support bigger herding animals such as cattle, goats, pigs, and poultry supply: thus most of the meat is usually roasted. Goat and sheep milk may also be utilized in a variety of dishes.

Because of the city's closeness to the Mediterranean Sea, seafood is easily accessible. Fresh herbs like garlic, marjoram, tarragon, thyme, oregano, shallots, parsley, basil, and cloves define Mediterranean cuisine.

The "Mediterranean Bowls Cookbook" is jam-packed with delectable Mediterranean dishes. The recipes given in the chapters are Spanish, French, and Greek. Begin reading this book to get the health advantages of Mediterranean Bowls cuisine.

Chapter 1: Spanish Bowls Recipes

1.1 Grilled Chicken Rice Bowl

Cooking Time: 50 minutes

Serving Size: 4

Ingredients:

Spanish Rice

- 1 teaspoon lime juice
- Salt and pepper
- ½ teaspoon cumin
- 1 teaspoon tomato paste
- ¼ teaspoon oregano
- ½ teaspoon paprika
- 5 cherry tomatoes
- 1/8 cup cilantro
- 1 tablespoon butter
- 1 clove garlic
- 1 cup rice
- 2 cups water

Method:

1. Add the butter and garlic to a saucepan over medium heat.
2. Cook for thirty seconds until aromatic, then add the tomatoes and continue cooking.
3. Add the rice and parsley and cook for 3 minutes in the oil.

4. Get another pot out and add the tomato paste, cumin, water, oregano, lime juice, paprika, salt, and pepper while the rice is heating in the pan.

5. Reduce the heat to low and continue to cook.

6. Add the sliced grilled chicken and garnishes on the top.

1.2 Mexican Rice Rainbow Bowls

Cooking Time: 15 minutes

Serving Size: 4

Ingredients:

Vegetarian Mexican Rice

- Grilled vegetables
- Mango
- Cilantro
- Hot sauce
- Romaine lettuce
- Lime
- 15 oz. Beans
- Tomato
- Salsa
- Sliced avocado
- Bell peppers
- Jalapeno
- A pinch of salt

Method:

1. Fill separate bowls with rice.
2. Toss in the seasoned beans.
3. Arrange your preferred toppings on top and enjoy!

1.3 Chicken Burrito Bowl

Cooking Time: 1 hour

Serving Size: 4

Ingredients:

- ¼ cup cilantro
- 2 cups cheddar cheese
- ⅔ cup corn
- ⅔ cup black beans
- 2 cups salsa
- 2 teaspoon seasoning mix
- Kosher salt and pepper
- 4 cups brown rice
- 1 lime
- 2 chicken breasts
- ½ cup red onion

Method:

1. Mix onions with fresh lemon juice from 2 lemon slices in a small bowl.
2. Pat dry the chicken breasts.
3. Grill over medium-high heat in an oiled grill pan.
4. Remove the chicken from the heat for at least five minutes before dicing it.
5. Mix cooked black beans, cilantro, rice, taco seasonings, salsa, corn, onion/lime combination, and chicken in a large pan.
6. To heat thoroughly, cook on medium-high.

7. Serve with a sprinkling of cheese on top.

1.4 Mushroom Fajita Bowls

Cooking Time: 30 minutes

Serving Size: 2

Ingredients:

- 2 tablespoons olive oil
- Salt
- ¼ oz. cilantro
- 3 tablespoons sour cream
- 1 red onion
- 1 mango
- 1 jalapeño
- 2 teaspoon chimichurri blends
- 7 oz. Spanish rice
- 3 garlic cloves
- 1 lime
- 8 oz. cremini mushrooms

Method:

1. Preheat the oven to 375 degrees Fahrenheit.
2. In a large mixing bowl, combine the lime juice, red onion, chimichurri mixture, garlic, olive oil, cremini mushrooms, and salt.
3. Toss and set aside for 10 minutes to marinate.
4. On a baking sheet, spread out the marinated mushrooms and onions.
5. Roast until the mushrooms are soft and the onions are lightly browned.

6. Fill a small saucepan halfway with water and bring to a boil.

7. Remove the saucepan from the heat, add the Spanish Rice, cover, and set aside eight minutes.

8. Toss the mango slaw with the remaining mango, red onion, and sliced jalapeno in a medium bowl.

9. Add sour cream on top of mushroom fajita dishes and garnish with cilantro leaves and stems.

1.5 Fiesta Bowl with Mexican Rice

Cooking Time: 30 minutes

Serving Size: 5

Ingredients:

- Avocado
- Salsa
- Organic black beans
- Mexican blend cheese
- Carnitas
- Frozen roasted corn
- 2 ½ cups chicken broth
- 1 can tomato sauce
- 1 ½ teaspoon sea salt
- 4 cloves garlic
- 2 cups jasmine rice
- ½ teaspoon cumin
- ½ sweet onion
- 2 tablespoon butter

Method:

1. Heat the oil in a big heavy-bottomed pan or Dutch oven until it sparkles.

2. Add the onion and cook for 2 minutes, or until softened.

3. Add the rice and toss to coat all of the grains with oil.

4. Stir often until the rice starts to brown.

5. Stir in the salt, cumin, and garlic for approximately 1 minute, or until fragrant.

6. Bring to a boil with the broth and tomato sauce.

7. Cover and cook for approximately 15 minutes or until all liquid has been absorbed.

1.6 Ground Turkey Taco Bowls

Cooking Time: 15 minutes

Serving Size: 4

Ingredients:
For the Turkey Tacos

- 2 tablespoons avocado oil
- ¼ cup apple cider vinegar
- ½ cup chicken broth
- 1 teaspoon chipotle powder
- 3 tablespoon tomato paste
- 1 teaspoon oregano
- 1 teaspoon salt
- 1 teaspoon paprika
- 2 teaspoon garlic
- 3 teaspoon cumin
- 2 teaspoon coriander
- 1/3 cup white onion
- 1 tablespoon chili powder
- 1.5 lbs. turkey

For the Cauliflower Rice

- ½ cup chicken broth
- Fresh cilantro
- 1 teaspoon salt
- 2 tablespoon tomato paste

- 3 cloves garlic

- 1 teaspoon cumin

- 1 tablespoon olive oil

- ½ cup onion

- 1 large cauliflower

Method:

1. Preheat the oven to 350°F and a large pan to medium heat.

2. Add the onion and oil once the pan is heated.

3. Allow simmering for another 2-3 minutes before adding the ground turkey or beef.

4. Continue stirring to ensure that the meat cooks evenly.

5. Add spices to the meat.

6. Combine the apple cider vinegar, tomato paste, and vegetable broth in a mixing bowl.

7. Allow cooking for 3-5 minutes.

8. Preheat a large skillet over medium-high heat.

9. Sauté for 3 minutes with the onion.

10. Combine the salt, cauliflower rice, and cumin in a mixing bowl.

11. Toss the vegetable mixture around to coat it.

12. Increase the heat to moderately high and add the tomato paste, followed by ¼ cup broth.

13. On the bottom, layer the cauliflower rice, then top it with taco meat.

1.7 Zucchini Spanish Rice Burrito Bowls

Cooking Time: 45 minutes

Serving Size: 6

Ingredients:

Zucchini Spanish Rice

- 1 medium zucchini
- 1 cup shredded cheddar
- 1 cup chicken broth
- 1 cup salsa
- ¼ teaspoon chili powder
- ¼ teaspoon smoked paprika
- 1 cup uncooked rice
- ½ teaspoon cumin
- 3 tablespoons yellow onion
- 2 teaspoon garlic
- 1 tablespoon olive oil

Chicken and Mushrooms

- ½ teaspoon seasoned salt
- 8 oz. mushrooms
- ½ teaspoon cumin
- ½ teaspoon garlic powder
- 1 teaspoon chili powder
- ½ teaspoon oregano
- 2 lbs. chicken breast
- 2 tablespoon olive oil

Method:

1. In a large pan, heat the olive oil for one minute over medium heat.

2. Cook for 3 minutes after adding the onion.

3. Continue cooking while stirring in the rice and seasonings.

4. Bring to a boil with the chicken broth and salsa.

5. Prepare the chicken as well as the mushrooms.

6. Add cumin, garlic powder, chili powder, oregano, and salt to season the chicken.

7. Over medium-high heat, brown the seasoned chicken.

8. Cook for eight minutes in the same skillet with the chopped mushrooms.

9. Replace the lid and let the skillet covered off the heat for five minutes, or until the cheese has melted and the zucchini is soft.

1.8 Spanish Rice and Beans Bowl

Cooking Time: 50 minutes

Serving Size: 6

Ingredients:

- 3 cups vegetable broth
- 1/3 cup green olives
- 1 can tomatoes
- 2 cans kidney beans
- ¼ teaspoon cayenne pepper
- 2 cups white rice
- 1 teaspoon oregano
- ½ teaspoon black pepper
- 1 ¼ teaspoon kosher salt
- 1 teaspoon chili powder
- 3 garlic cloves
- 1 ½ teaspoon paprika
- 1 yellow onion
- 2 tablespoons olive oil

Parsley Oil

- ½ teaspoon lemon zest
- 3 tablespoons olive oil
- 3 tablespoon parsley leaves

Method:

1. In a large skillet with a fitting cover, heat the oil over medium heat.
2. Cook for 5 minutes or until the onion is softened.

3. Cook 60 seconds, often stirring, until oregano, garlic, salt, black pepper, chili powder, paprika, and cayenne are fragrant.

4. Cook for 2 minutes, or until rice is slightly transparent.

5. Combine the beans, tomatoes, and broth in a mixing bowl.

6. Bring the mixture to a boil, lower to low heat and cook for approximately half an hour.

7. Meantime, make parsley oil by whisking together lemon zest, parsley, lemon juice, and olive oil in a small bowl.

Chapter 2: Italian Bowls Recipes

2.1 Italian Power Pasta Bowl

Cooking Time: 40 minutes

Serving Size: 16

Ingredients:

- 1 cup pesto sauce
- 3 cups alfredo sauce
- 4 12-ounce penne pasta
- 4 cups marinara sauce
- 60 small shrimp
- 5 chicken breasts

Method:

1. Assemble a dish with noodles and a variety of toppings.
2. Add your favorite sauce and mix with prepared ingredients!

2.2 Meatball Italian Bowl

Cooking Time: 30 minutes

Serving Size: 4

Ingredients:

- 24 ounces marinara sauce
- Parmesan cheese
- 12 oz. meatballs
- 1 head broccoli
- 1 cup penne pasta

Method:

1. Divide the ingredients evenly among the four bowls.

2. Clean, cut, and toss your broccoli in olive oil to roast it.

3. Season with a pinch of salt and pepper.

4. Bake for 5-10 minutes on a baking sheet at 375°F until tender.

5. Cook the pasta as directed on the box.

6. Heat the meatballs until cooked.

7. Toss the spaghetti into the mixing bowl.

8. In a mixing dish, place the meatballs.

9. Toss the roasted broccoli into the mixing bowl.

10. Pour in the marinara sauce.

2.3 Italian Minestrone Bowls

Cooking Time: 50 minutes

Serving Size: 6

Ingredients:

- 1 vegetable combination
- 1 can cannellini beans
- 1 teaspoon fresh garlic
- 2 chicken broth
- ½-pound chicken breast
- 1 tablespoon seasoning
- 1 tablespoon butter
- 8 ounces spaghetti

Method:

1. Cook the pasta as directed on the box.
2. Meanwhile, in a 4-quart pot, heat the butter until it foams; add the chicken, herb seasoning, and garlic.
3. Cook, stirring periodically, over medium-high heat.
4. Combine the veggies, broth, and beans in a large mixing bowl.
5. Cook for another 8-10 minutes, stirring periodically.
6. Remove from heat and set aside for 15 minutes to cool.
7. To serve, divide spaghetti equally among six separate dishes and top with chicken mixture.

2.4 Italian Polenta Bowl

Cooking Time: 30 minutes

Serving Size: 6

Ingredients:

Toppings

- Jarred roasted red peppers
- Parmesan cheese
- Artichoke hearts
- Black or green olives
- Meatballs
- Red onions

Polenta

- ½ teaspoon kosher salt
- ½ teaspoon pepper
- ¼ cup parmesan cheese
- 1/3 cup ricotta cheese
- 1 ½ cups cooking polenta
- ¼ cup tomatoes
- 3 cloves garlic
- 4 cups chicken broth
- 2 teaspoons Italian seasoning
- 1 tablespoon olive oil

Method:

1. Cook meatballs or sausage according to the package directions.

2. Over low heat, heat a medium-sized saucepan.

3. Pour in the olive oil.

4. Combine the Italian seasoning and red pepper flakes in a mixing bowl.

5. Sauté for 30 seconds after adding the garlic.

6. Place the chicken broth in the pot.

7. Cook for 3 to 5 minutes after slowly whisking in the polenta.

8. Add the ricotta cheese, sun-dried tomatoes, Parmesan cheese, and salt and pepper after the polenta has hardened.

9. Serve with cooked meatballs or sausage on top.

2.5 Italian Bread Bowls

Cooking Time: 1 hour 75 minutes

Serving Size: 8

Ingredients:

- 1 egg white
- 1 tablespoon water
- 7 cups all-purpose flour
- 1 tablespoon cornmeal
- 2 teaspoons salt
- 2 tablespoons vegetable oil
- 2 ½ cups warm water
- 2 (.25 ounce) packages of dry yeast

Method:

1. Dissolve yeast in warm water in a large mixing bowl.
2. Allow 10 minutes for the mixture to become creamy.
3. Toss the yeast mixture with the oil, salt, and 5 cups flour and mix thoroughly.
4. ½ cup at a time, stir in the residual flour.
5. Make a 4-inch round loaf out of each portion.
6. Preheat the oven to 400 degrees Fahrenheit.
7. Whisk together the egg white and one tablespoon water; lightly rub half of the egg wash over the loaves.
8. Bake for 15 minutes in a preheated oven.

9. Brush the remaining egg mixture over the top and
   bake for another five to ten minutes, or until
   golden.

2.6 Italian Chicken Meal Prep Bowls

Cooking Time: 1 hour

Serving Size: 4

Ingredients:

- 2 tablespoons olive oil
- 2-4 cups cooked rice
- 1 medium zucchini
- 2 teaspoon garlic
- 1 small red onion
- 1 cup plum tomatoes
- 0.91 kg chicken breasts
- 1 ½ cup broccoli florets
- 2 teaspoon thyme
- 1 teaspoon paprika
- 2 teaspoon marjoram
- 2 teaspoon rosemary
- ½ teaspoon pepper
- 2 teaspoon basil
- 1 teaspoon salt

Method:

1. Preheat the oven to 232 degrees Fahrenheit.
2. Combine thyme, rosemary, salt, marjoram, basil, pepper, and paprika in a small bowl.
3. In a baking dish, combine the chicken and vegetables.

4. Scatter all the seasonings and garlic evenly over the meat and vegetables.

5. Sprinkle with olive oil.

6. Bake for 15-twenty minutes, or until meat is cooked and vegetables have charred slightly.

7. On top of the rice, evenly distribute the chicken and vegetables.

8. Cover and keep in the fridge for 2- 5 days or serve for supper!

2.7 Italian Meatball Quinoa Bowls

Cooking Time: 20 minutes

Serving Size: 4

Ingredients:

- 1 jar marinara sauce
- 2 cups cooked quinoa
- 1 cup breadcrumbs
- ½ cup water
- ½ cup grated Parmigiano
- ¼ cup Italian parsley
- 1 ½ pounds ground beef
- 2 large eggs
- 2 cloves garlic
- Pinch red pepper
- 1 large onion
- Salt, to taste
- Extra-virgin olive oil

Method:

1. In a big pan, heat the olive oil.
2. Combine the salt, onion, and garlic in a mixing bowl.
3. Cook until the onions are very tender and browning.
4. Remove from the oven and set aside to cool.

5. Combine the onion combination, red pepper, ground beef, breadcrumbs, eggs, parsley, Parmigiano-Reggiano, and water in a large mixing bowl.

6. Form the meat mixture into balls of the appropriate size.

7. In the same pan, heat some more olive oil.

8. Cook for 15 minutes over medium heat or until browned on both sides.

9. Cook for another 5 minutes after adding the marinara sauce.

2.8 Italian Sausage and Broccoli Bowls

Cooking Time: 30 minutes

Serving Size: 4

Ingredients:

- 2 cups grains
- 4 oz. mozzarella cheese
- 1 teaspoon sugar
- 4 Italian sausages
- 2 pints grape tomatoes
- 2 garlic cloves
- 1 tablespoon olive oil
- Salt and pepper
- 1 bunch broccoli

Method:

1. Preheat the oven to 475 degrees Fahrenheit.
2. Chop one bunch of broccolis into florets, put out on a large baking sheet.
3. Roast until browned, tossing with kosher salt, olive oil, and pepper.
4. Cook three to four Italian sausages in a nonstick pan over medium heat.
5. In a pan, combine 2 quarts of grape tomatoes, two peeled and crushed cloves of garlic and sugar.
6. Cook on a medium-high heat setting.
7. Slice the sausages and serve with broccoli.

Chapter 3: Mediterranean Bowls Recipes

3.1 Mediterranean Bulgur Bowl

Cooking Time: 30 minutes

Serving Size: 4

Ingredients:

- 2 tablespoons fresh mint
- 2 tablespoons lemon juice
- ½ cup feta cheese
- ¼ cup hummus
- 2 cups cherry tomatoes
- 1 small red onion
- 1 can garbanzo beans
- 6 ounces baby spinach
- 1 cup bulgur
- ¼ teaspoon salt
- 2 cups water
- ½ teaspoon cumin

Method:

1. Combine the first four ingredients in a stockpot and bring to a boil.
2. Reduce heat to low and cook, covered, for 10-12 minutes, or until vegetables are soft.
3. Heat through the garbanzo beans.
4. Remove from the fire and add the spinach.

5. Allow it to sit for a few minutes, covered until the spinach has wilted.

6. Combine the remaining ingredients in a mixing bowl.

3.2 Mediterranean Tilapia Power Bowls

Cooking Time: 45 minutes

Serving Size: 4

Ingredients:

Tilapia Fillets

- ½ teaspoon red pepper flakes
- ½ teaspoon cumin powder
- ½ teaspoon pepper
- 1 tablespoon oregano leaves
- Juice from ½ lemon
- 1 teaspoon salt
- 4 garlic cloves
- 3 tablespoons olive oil
- 4 Tilapia fillets

Lemon Herb Tahini Dressing

- 6 tablespoons cold water
- 1 teaspoon ground cumin
- Juice from a lemon
- 2 teaspoon salt
- ½ cup tahini paste

Greek Power Bowls

- 1 cup pickled red onions
- Pita bread for serving
- 2 cups chickpeas

* 1 cup feta cheese
* 2 cups cherry tomatoes
* 2 cups cucumbers
* 2 cups quinoa

Method:

1. Whisk the lime juice, tahini paste, cold water, salt, and powdered cumin in a small bowl.
2. Season with more salt or spices.
3. Whisk together the garlic cloves, sunflower oil, and other spices in a small bowl.
4. Marinate the Tilapia fillets in the marinade.
5. Refrigerate for half an hour after covering.
6. Cook for 2–3 minutes on each side in a grill pan or large skillet with a sprinkle of olive oil.
7. Drizzle lemon herb tahini dressing over each bowl of marinated Tilapia fillets.

3.3 Mediterranean Buddha Bowl

Cooking Time: 1 hour

Serving Size: 4

Ingredients:

- 1 cup red onion
- 15 oz. chickpeas
- 4 oz. quinoa
- 2 cup cucumber
- 1 tablespoon lemon
- 1 teaspoon zaatar seasoning
- 1 teaspoon garlic powder
- 1 tablespoon tahini
- 4 tablespoons olive oil
- 4 cup kale
- 1 medium eggplant

Method:

1. Preheat oven to 425 degrees Fahrenheit.
2. Combine the oil, kale, and garlic powder in a separate baking dish.
3. After thoroughly mixing, put the kale and eggplant in the oven.
4. Roast the kale and eggplant until they are nicely browned and cooked.
5. Combine the leftover olive oil, lime juice, tahini, and za'atar in a small bowl.
6. To make Buddha bowls, divide the grains among four bowls, top with roasted kale, peel the eggplant, and split the bowls.

3.4 Mediterranean Hummus Bowl

Cooking Time: 40 minutes

Serving Size: 4

Ingredients:

For the Hummus

- 2-3 tablespoon cold water
- salt, pepper
- ½ teaspoon ground cumin
- ½ teaspoon salt
- 2 tablespoons olive oil
- 1-2 garlic cloves
- ¼ cup lemon juice
- ¼ cup tahini
- 8.8 oz. chickpeas

For the Bowl

- Some black olives
- Some fried pimientos
- ½ cucumber
- 3.5 oz. feta cheese
- 9 oz. small tomatoes
- 1 small red onion
- 1 ¼ cups water
- 1.8 oz. baby spinach leaves
- Olive oil

* 5.3 oz. quinoa

* ½ teaspoon onion powder

* ¼ teaspoon paprika powder

* ½ teaspoon garlic powder

* 1 can chickpeas

Method:

1. In a food processor, combine the tahini and lime juice and process for one minute.

2. Mix in the spice, olive oil, garlic, and salt until smooth.

3. Add half of the chickpeas to the food processor/mixer and pulse for another moment, or until creamy.

4. Add the rest chickpeas and stir with the spices for another 1-2 minutes to get a smooth paste.

5. Preheat the oven to 390 degrees Fahrenheit.

6. Roast chickpeas for 20-25 minutes, or until well browned.

7. Cook the quinoa according to package instructions while the chickpeas roast.

8. Whisk together some olive oil and fresh lemon juice to make the dressing, then season with salt and pepper to taste.

3.5 Mediterranean Chickpea Salad Bowl

Cooking Time: 10 minutes

Serving Size: 4

Ingredients:

Dressing

- ½ teaspoon agave
- Salt to taste
- 2 tablespoons red wine vinegar
- ½ teaspoon dried oregano
- 2 tablespoon lemon
- 3 tablespoons olive oil
- 2 garlic cloves

Mediterranean Chickpea Salad

- 1/3 cup red onion
- ¼ cup feta crumbles
- 1 cup cherry tomatoes
- ¾ cup parsley leaves
- 1 cup cucumbers
- 15.5 oz. can chickpeas

For the Bowl

- 1 garlic hummus
- 1 warm pita bread
- ½ cup arugula
- ½ cup quinoa

Method:

1. Toss chickpeas, parsley, cucumbers, tomatoes, onion, and feta in a large mixing bowl.

2. To make the dressing, combine the oregano, minced garlic, agave, olive oil, lemon juice, red wine vinegar, and salt in a small container.

3. Toss the salad with the dressing.

3.6 Mediterranean Power Bowls with Red Pepper Sauce

Cooking Time: 30 minutes

Serving Size: 4

Ingredients:

- 3 oz. feta cheese
- Fresh basil and lemon wedges
- 2 tablespoon rice vinegar
- ¼ teaspoon black pepper
- 1 avocado
- ½ cup red onion
- ½ teaspoon ground cumin
- ½ English cucumber
- ½ teaspoon kosher salt
- 1 (15-oz. can) chickpeas
- 1 cup dry quinoa

Red Pepper Sauce

- ¼ teaspoon red pepper flakes
- ¼ teaspoon kosher salt

- 1 garlic clove

- 1 teaspoon paprika

- ¼ cup olive oil

- 1 (12-oz.) jarred peppers

Method:

1. In a skillet, combine the water, quinoa, and salt.

2. Bring to a boil, lower to low heat, cover, and simmer for 15 - 20 minutes.

3. Remove from the heat, mix in the chickpeas and cumin, cover, and set aside until ready to serve.

4. Prepare the avocado-cucumber salad while the quinoa is cooking by mixing vinegar, cucumber, red onion, avocado, remaining salt, and black pepper in a bowl.

5. In a blender, combine all of the ingredients for red pepper sauce.

6. Divide the quinoa and chickpea mixture equally among four bowls.

3.7 Mediterranean Steak and Quinoa Bowl

Cooking Time: 1 hour

Serving Size: 4

Ingredients:

Marinade

- ¼ teaspoon salt
- 2 teaspoons Greek seasoning
- ½ teaspoon Dijon mustard
- ¼ teaspoon honey
- 2 ½ tablespoons olive oil
- 2 ½ tablespoons red wine vinegar

Bowl

- ⅔ cup tomatoes
- ½ cup cucumber
- 16 cups baby spinach
- 3 cups quinoa
- 1-pound sirloin steak

Tzatziki Sauce

- 1/8 teaspoon kosher salt
- ¼ teaspoon black pepper
- 1 ½ teaspoon olive oil
- 1 tablespoon dill weed
- 1 tablespoon lemon juice
- 1 teaspoon lemon zest

- ¼ cup cucumber

- ½ cup Greek yogurt

Method:

1. In a small dish, mix the marinade ingredients.

2. Half of the marinade should be placed in a zip-top plastic bag, and the other half should be saved for basting.

3. Toss the meat in the bag with the Greek seasoning.

4. For sirloin, marinate for 15 minutes to 2 hours.

5. Preheat a grill pan over "MEDIUM-HIGH" heat on the stove.

6. Place steak on the hot grill pan and cook for 10-12 minutes for medium-rare.

7. Cook quinoa according to package directions while steaming spinach in a saucepan.

8. In a mixing bowl, combine all of the ingredients for the Tzatziki sauce.

9. Tzatziki sauce and feta cheese go on top of the bowls.

3.8 Mediterranean Cauliflower Rice Tabbouleh Bowls

Cooking Time: 40 minutes

Serving Size: 4

Ingredients:

- 1 cup hummus
- ¼ cup hemp hearts
- 12 green olives
- 1 jar artichoke hearts
- 4 green onions
- 1 16 oz. package tofu
- ½ cup parsley
- 1 cup cilantro
- Himalayan sea salt
- Black pepper
- 1 medium cauliflower
- 2 cups tomatoes
- Juice from 1 lemon
- 1 red bell pepper

Method:

1. Preheat the oven to 400 degrees Fahrenheit.

2. Pulse the cauliflower in a food processor.

3. In a large mixing bowl, combine the grape tomatoes, red bell pepper, parsley and green onion, cilantro, and lemon juice.

4. Stir in a sprinkle of Himalayan sea salt and black pepper to blend the flavors.

5. Make your herbed tofu in the meantime.

6. Bake for 10 to 15 minutes, or until vegetables are soft.

7. To make the bowls, divide the cauliflower rice and herbed baked tofu, then top with fresh parsley.

3.9 Mediterranean Lentil and Grain Bowls

Cooking Time: 1 hour

Serving Size: 4

Ingredients:

- ½ teaspoon red pepper flakes
- ½ teaspoon whole peppercorns
- 1 tablespoon maple syrup
- 1 ½ teaspoon fine sea salt
- ¾ cup water
- ½ cup apple cider vinegar
- 1 red onion

Farro

- Freshly cracked black pepper
- 2 garlic cloves
- Kosher salt
- 2 bay leaves
- 2 ½ cups water
- 1 cup (180g) farro

Creamy Mediterranean Lentils

- 2 tablespoons tahini
- 3 teaspoons tamari
- Kosher salt
- Black pepper to taste
- 2 ⅔ cup vegetable broth

* 1 cup green lentils

* 1 teaspoon cumin seeds

* 6 garlic cloves

* 1 tablespoon olive oil

Classic Hummus

* Freshly cracked black pepper

* 6 tablespoons ice water

* 1 teaspoon cumin

* 1 teaspoon kosher salt

* 1 medium lemon

* 2 garlic cloves

* 1/3 cup tahini

* 1 (15-ounce) can chickpeas

Method:

1. Combine the salt, boiling water, red pepper flakes, maple syrup, vinegar, and peppercorns in a large mixing bowl.

2. Stir until the sugar is completely dissolved.

3. Add the olive oil to a large pan and heat over medium heat.

4. Cook until the garlic and cumin seeds are aromatic.

5. After that, add the lentils and the vegetable broth.

6. Reduce the heat to low and whisk in the tahini and tamari until well combined.

7. In a medium saucepan, add the water, sprinkle with salt, and bring to a boil.

8. Combine the farro and spices in a mixing bowl.

9. Mix the chickpeas for 2 - 3 minutes in a food processor.

10. Combine the garlic, tahini, cumin, lemon juice, and salt in a mixing bowl.

11. Fill a serving dish halfway with hummus.

3.10 Mediterranean Salmon Bowl

Cooking Time: 25 minutes

Serving Size: 4

Ingredients:

For the Salmon

- ½ teaspoon salt
- 1/8 teaspoon pepper
- 1 lemon
- 2 teaspoon dried dill
- 3 tablespoons olive oil
- 16 oz. of salmon

For the Bowls

- 1 teaspoon of spice
- 2 garlic cloves
- ¼ cup olive oil
- 1 lemon
- 5 green onions
- ¼ cup fresh parsley
- ½ cup Kalamata olives

- ½ English cucumber
- 1 cup feta cheese
- ¼ cup red peppers
- 1-pint tomatoes
- 1 5 oz. lettuce

Method:

1. Preheat the oven to 400 degrees Fahrenheit.
2. Place the fish on a baking sheet and set it aside.
3. Cook the fish for 15-20 minutes in the oven.
4. Remove the salmon from the oven and place it in a dish, flaking it into big chunks.
5. Divide ingredients four bowls.
6. Toss the salmon pieces into each dish.

3.11 Mediterranean Quinoa Bowls with Salad

Cooking Time: 15 minutes

Serving Size: 2

Ingredients:

- ¼ cup kalamata olives
- ¼ cup feta cheese
- ½ cup cucumber
- ¼ cup red onion
- ½ cup chickpeas
- ¼ cup tomatoes
- 2 cups arugula
- ½ cup dry quinoa

Tahini Dressing

- ¼ teaspoon dill
- ¼ teaspoon oregano
- ⅛ teaspoon pepper
- ¼ teaspoon garlic powder
- ½ tablespoon apple cider vinegar
- ⅛ teaspoon salt
- 1 tablespoon olive oil
- 1 tablespoon balsamic vinegar
- 3 tablespoon lemon juice
- 1 tablespoon tahini

Method:

1. Follow the package directions for cooking quinoa.

2. In each bowl, combine all ingredients, including the sun-dried tomatoes, quinoa, and crushed feta cheese.

3. In a small container, combine all of the dressing ingredients.

4. Shake the container with the lid on until everything is well mixed.

3.12 Avocado Mediterranean Bowl

Cooking Time: 25 minutes

Serving Size: 4

Ingredients:

- ¼ cup olives
- ¼ cup red onion
- 2 cup tomatoes
- 1 cup feta
- 2 cup cucumber
- 2 cup parsley
- 2 cup chickpeas
- 4 cup bulger

Avocado Hummus

- 2 garlic cloves
- Salt and pepper
- 3 teaspoons avocado oil
- 2 teaspoon lemon juice
- 1 avocado
- ½ cup chickpeas

Lemon Vinaigrette

- 1 teaspoon Dijon mustard
- Salt and pepper, to taste
- 2 teaspoons avocado oil
- ¼ cup lemon juice

Method:

1. Combine avocado, chickpeas, lemon juice, avocado oil, and finely chopped garlic in a blender.

2. Blend until smooth, then season with salt and pepper to taste.

3. Add Dijon mustard, lemon juice, avocado oil, and salt & pepper to taste to a medium mixing bowl.

4. Stir until everything is thoroughly mixed.

5. Distribute ingredients equally in large mixing bowls.

3.13 Mediterranean Quinoa Bowls with Roasted Chickpeas

Cooking Time: 30 minutes

Serving Size: 4

Ingredients:

For Bowls

- ½ teaspoon salt
- 4 cups baby salad greens
- 4 tablespoons parsley
- Juice of 1 lemon
- 1-pint tomatoes
- ¼ red onion
- 1 English cucumber

For Roasted Chickpeas

- ¼ teaspoon salt
- 1 teaspoon olive oil
- ¼ teaspoon turmeric
- ¼ teaspoon garlic powder
- 1 teaspoon cumin
- ½ teaspoon oregano
- 1 can chickpeas

For the Citrus Tahini Sauce

- ½ teaspoon kosher salt
- ¼ teaspoon black pepper

- 2 tablespoons lemon juice

- 1 clove garlic

- 1/3 cup water

- 1/3 cup tahini

For Quinoa

- 1 ½ cups vegetable broth

- Salt and black pepper

- 1 cup dry quinoa

- 1 tablespoon olive oil

Method:

1. Preheat the oven to 400 degrees Fahrenheit.

2. In a mixing bowl, combine the spices, chickpeas, and olive oil; toss well.

3. In an equal layer, spread them out on the prepared baking sheet.

4. Roast for fifteen minutes, then mix in the chickpeas and roast for another five to ten minutes.

5. Sauté for two or three minutes with the quinoa.

6. Season with salt and pepper to taste.

7. Place all of the ingredients in the bowl of a food processor or blender to create the sauce.

8. Continuously process until everything is properly mixed.

3.14 Mediterranean Meatball Bowls

Cooking Time: 50 minutes

Serving Size: 2

Ingredients:

- 1 cup uncooked farro
- ¼ cup feta cheese
- Canned chickpeas
- 1 cup cherry tomatoes
- ½ cup hummus
- 4 cups baby spinach
- 1 large cucumber
- 1 teaspoon smoked paprika
- Pinch salt and black pepper
- 2 teaspoons fresh dill
- 1 tablespoon red wine vinegar
- ⅓ cup onion
- 1 tablespoon oregano
- 1 lb. ground beef
- 2 cloves garlic
- 3 cups water or broth

Method:

1. Preheat the oven to 425 degrees Fahrenheit.

2. To make the meatballs, combine all of the ingredients in a mixing bowl.

3. Preheat oven to 350°F and bake for 15-20 minutes.

4. Chop the vegetables and prepare your favorite whole grain while the meatballs bake.

5. Assemble the dishes after the grains and meatballs are done.

3.15 Wild Rice Mediterranean Bowls

Cooking Time: 1 hour

Serving Size: 4

Ingredients:

Roasted Cauliflower

- 1 teaspoon cumin
- 1 teaspoon sumac
- 1 small cauliflower
- 2 teaspoons avocado oil

Rice

- 3 ½ cups water
- 1 cup wild rice

Salad

- 12 kalamata olives
- 2 Medjool dates
- 1 cup red cabbage
- 2 carrots
- 2 15.5-ounce cans of chickpeas
- 12 ounces cherry tomatoes
- 1 teaspoon olive oil
- 4 leaves of kale

Dressing

- 1 clove of garlic
- ½ teaspoon sea salt

- 2 teaspoons Dijon mustard

- 1 teaspoon dried oregano

- 3 tablespoons lemon juice

- 1 tablespoon red wine vinegar

- ½ cup olive oil

Method:

1. Preheat the oven to 400 degrees Fahrenheit.

2. In a 3-quart saucepan, bring wild rice and water to a boil.

3. Reduce the heat and cover.

4. Cook for 55 minutes, or until the vegetables are soft.

5. Prepare the cauliflower while the rice is cooking.

6. Combine sumac, avocado oil, and cumin in a medium mixing bowl.

7. Roast for 25-half an hour on the prepared baking sheet.

8. Shake the dressing ingredients vigorously in a container.

9. Massage for one minute with olive oil.

10. Make the bowls.

3.16 Mediterranean Bowl with Spicy Yogurt Sauce

Cooking Time: 30 minutes

Serving Size: 4

Ingredients:

- 1 watermelon radish
- 1 radish
- 1 heirloom carrot
- ½ cup baby kale
- 1 cup canned chickpeas
- 1 cup sugar snap peas
- 1 cup wild rice

Method:

1. Cook wild rice according to the package directions.

2. Combine lemon juice, Greek yogurt, cayenne, salt, spicy sauce, cumin, garlic, and pepper in a medium mixing bowl.

3. Half of the wild rice should be placed in each bowl, followed by watermelon, snap peas, carrots, kale, chickpeas, and radish.

4. Serve immediately with Spicy Yogurt Sauce on top.

3.17 Mediterranean Grain Bowls with Lentils and Chickpeas

Cooking Time: 10 minutes

Serving Size: 4

Ingredients:

- Handful olives
- Sprinkle feta cheese
- 2 avocados
- 1 cup parsley
- 2 cups tomatoes
- 2 shallots
- 2 cups lentils, brown
- 2 cups chickpeas
- 1 zucchini
- 2 cups farro
- Salt
- Olive oil

Dressing

- 1 teaspoon za'atar
- ½ teaspoon sumac
- 2 ½ teaspoon mustard
- Salt and pepper
- 1/3 cup olive oil
- 1 clove garlic

- 2 ½ tablespoon lemon juice

Method:

1. Heat olive oil in a nonstick pan or skillet over moderate flame.

2. Add the sliced zucchini and cook until cooked on both sides.

3. Season with a pinch of salt.

4. Fill a container halfway with the dressing ingredients.

5. Close the cover firmly and shake it vigorously.

6. In four dinner dishes, evenly distribute the lentils, cooked farro, and chickpeas.

3.18 Mediterranean Mezze Bowl

Cooking Time: 50 minutes

Serving Size: 4

Ingredients:

Quinoa Tabbouleh

- 1 cup cucumber
- 1½ cups cherry tomatoes
- 1 cup flat-leaf parsley
- 1 cup fresh mint leaves
- 1 teaspoon black pepper
- 1 cup scallions
- ¼ cup olive oil
- ½ teaspoon kosher salt
- ¼ cup lemon juice
- 1 cup quinoa

Easy Hummus

- ¼ teaspoon pepper
- 3 tablespoons olive oil
- 1 clove garlic
- ½ teaspoon salt
- ¼ cup water
- ½ teaspoon cumin
- ½ cup tahini
- 3 tablespoons fresh lemon juice
- 1 can chickpeas

Pickled Cucumbers

- ½ teaspoon red pepper

- 1 cucumber

- 4 teaspoons sugar

- 1 teaspoon soy sauce

- ¼ cup rice vinegar

Vegetables

- 2 yellow squash

- 2 red peppers

- 1 12 oz. bag brussels sprouts

Method:

1. In a food processor, combine all of the components except the olive oil.

2. While mixing, drizzle in the olive oil.

3. Whisk together olive oil, lemon juice, and salt in a small bowl.

4. Combine the prepared quinoa and the lemon juice dressing in a large mixing dish.

5. Add tomatoes, parsley, scallions, cucumber, and pepper.

6. Toss everything together.

7. Toss the cucumber slices in the vinegar mixture until they are well covered.

8. Preheat the oven to 400 degrees Fahrenheit.

9. Preheat oven to 350°F and bake for half an hour, or until vegetables are soft and slightly crunchy.

10. Roast peppers for 20-half an hour under a preheated broiler.

3.19 Mediterranean Rice Bowl with Rotisserie Chicken

Cooking Time: 2 hours

Serving Size: 4

Ingredients:

For the Salad

- ¼ teaspoon salt
- 1/8 teaspoon black pepper
- 1 tablespoon olive oil
- Juice of 1 lemon
- ¼ cup kalamata olives
- ¼ cup crumbled feta
- 2 plum tomatoes
- 1 English cucumber

For the Rice

- 1 cup brown rice
- 2 cups chicken broth

For the Chicken

- 1/8 teaspoon black pepper
- ¼ cup tzatziki sauce
- 1 teaspoon oregano
- ¼ teaspoon salt
- 1 teaspoon rosemary
- 1 teaspoon thyme
- 1 tablespoon olive oil

- 4 cups rotisserie chicken

- Juice of 1 lemon

- 1 clove garlic

Method:

1. Bring the chicken stock and rice to a boil in a medium saucepan over high heat.

2. Reduce the heat to medium-low and continue to cook.

3. Toss the tomatoes, cucumbers, and olives in a medium mixing bowl.

4. Toss in the salt, feta, lemon juice, oil, and pepper until everything is well combined.

5. In a medium saucepan, heat the oil over medium heat.

6. Cook, stirring periodically until the garlic is fragrant.

7. Toss in the lime juice, chicken, and seasonings to mix.

8. Cook for 5 minutes, or until the chicken is well heated.

3.20 Mediterranean Grain Bowls with Salmon

Cooking Time: 30 minutes

Serving Size: 6

Ingredients:

- ¼ cup basil leaves
- Pinch red pepper flakes
- ¼ cup red onion
- Zest and juice of 1 lemon
- 1 medium avocado
- ½ cup Kalamata olives
- 1 ½ cups cherry tomatoes
- Coarse salt and black pepper
- 4-ounces feta
- 1 ½ cups cucumber
- 6 fillets salmon
- ¼ cup olive oil
- 1 ½ cups quinoa

Method:

1. Follow the package instructions for quinoa preparation.
2. Preheat the oven to a low broiling setting.
3. Place the fish on a baking pan and bake it.
4. Season with salt and black pepper and drizzle with olive oil.
5. Cook for 5-7 minutes under the broiler.
6. To make the bowls, scoop grain into four separate dishes.

7. On top of the quinoa, scatter fish and feta pieces.

8. Place the other ingredients, as well as the cheese, on top.

3.21 Mediterranean Edamame Quinoa Bowl

Cooking Time: 12 minutes

Serving Size: 1

Ingredients:

Salad Bowl

- ¼ cup red onions
- 2 tablespoons pine nuts
- 10 Kalamata olives
- 1 small Persian cucumber
- 2 cups greens
- ½ cup cherry tomatoes
- ½ cup cooked quinoa
- ½ cup edamame

Mediterranean Vinaigrette

- Pinch red paprika
- ½ teaspoon oregano
- Pinch sea salt
- Pinch black pepper
- 1 ½ tablespoon red wine vinegar
- 1 clove garlic
- 1 tablespoon olive oil

Method:

1. Greens should be placed in one big dish.

2. Arrange cooked quinoa, cherry tomatoes, cucumbers, red onions, Kalamata olives, edamame, and peanuts on top of the greens.

3. Whisk together all the ingredients for the vinaigrette.

4. Drizzle the dressing evenly over the salad bowl.

3.22 Mediterranean Hummus Bowl with Chickpeas and Soft-Boiled Egg

Cooking Time: 5 minutes

Serving Size: 1

Ingredients:

- 1 soft-boiled egg
- ¼ cup tabbouleh salad
- ½ cup eggplant
- ½ cup chickpeas
- ½ cup hummus

Method:

1. In the base of a small bowl, pour the hummus.

2. Add chickpeas, egg, eggplant, and tabbouleh salad on the top.

3.23 Mediterranean Plant Protein Power Bowl

Cooking Time: 25 minutes

Serving Size: 2

Ingredients:

- ½ lemon juiced
- 1 teaspoon red wine vinegar
- ½ avocado
- 2 tablespoons olive oil
- ½ cucumber sliced
- ¼ red onion
- ¼ cup kalamata olives
- ¼ cup hummus
- 2 cups spinach
- ½ cup cherry tomatoes
- 2 cups vegetable broth
- 1 cup quinoa uncooked

Method:

1. In a large saucepan on the stove, combine the quinoa and vegetable broth.

2. Bring to a boil, then turn down to low heat.

3. Cook for another 10 to 15 minutes on low heat, covered.

4. In a large mixing bowl, combine cherry tomatoes, spinach leaves, cucumber, red onion, olives, hummus, avocado, and quinoa.

5. Drizzle lemon juice, olive oil, and red wine vinegar over the top.

3.24 Copy Cat Cava Mediterranean Grain Bowl

Cooking Time: 15 minutes

Serving Size: 1

Ingredients:

- Extra mint
- Squeeze of lemon
- 25g cabbage
- 40g hummus
- 25g pickled red onion
- 14g feta
- 100g Greek salsa
- 30g tzatziki
- 75g arugula
- 100g grilled Greek chicken
- ½ cup brown rice

Method:

1. In a large mixing dish, combine brown rice and arugula.

2. Serve hummus, grilled Greek Chicken, pickled onion, Greek Salsa, tzatziki, and cabbage on top.

3. Extra mint, feta, and a touch of lemon are optional.

3.25 Mediterranean Bowl with Lemon Dressing

Cooking Time: 15 minutes

Serving Size: 8

Ingredients:

- 3½ cups water
- 2 cups kale
- 2 cups quinoa cooked

Tahini Dressing

- 2 tablespoon water
- Salt to taste
- 3 tablespoon lemon juice
- 2 teaspoons olive oil
- 2 tablespoon tahini

Protein

- 2 teaspoons Kosher salt
- 1 teaspoon black pepper
- 1 tablespoon olive oil
- 2 ½ lb. halibut

Mediterranean Seasoning Blend

- 1 tablespoon cumin
- 1 tablespoon Kosher salt
- 3 tablespoon oregano
- 1 tablespoon red pepper

- 3 tablespoon sesame seeds

Fixings

- 1 jarred peppers

- 1 avocado

- 2 cups cherry tomatoes

- 1 can artichoke hearts

- 2 small cucumbers

Method:

1. Prepare the quinoa according to the package instructions.

2. Preheat the oven to 400 degrees Fahrenheit.

3. Place the fish on a baking sheet lined with parchment paper.

4. Season the halibut with salt and pepper, then season both sides with the Mediterranean spice mix.

5. Over the fish, drizzle the olive oil.

6. Cook the salmon for 10 minutes in the oven.

7. To make the dressing, combine all of the ingredients in a mixing bowl.

3.26 Mediterranean Chicken and Rice Pita Bowls

Cooking Time: 20 minutes

Serving Size: 4

Ingredients:

- 1 cup chicken
- Lemon wedges
- ½ cup onion
- 2 teaspoons za'atar
- 2 teaspoons garlic
- 1 tablespoon olive oil
- 1 tablespoon lemon juice
- 1 tablespoon water
- 4 pita bread rounds
- 2 tablespoons tahini paste
- Non-stick cooking spray

Method:

1. Follow the package instructions for cooking rice.
2. Preheat the oven to 425 degrees Fahrenheit.
3. To make a bowl, press pitas into oven-safe bowls or cups.
4. Bake for 20 minutes on a baking sheet.
5. Combine the lemon juice, water, tahini, and garlic in a small bowl.
6. Stir until the mixture is completely smooth.
7. In a medium skillet, heat the oil over medium heat.

8. Sauté for 1 minute with the remaining garlic and onions.

9. Combine the chicken, za'atar, and rice in a mixing bowl.

10. Sauté for another 2 minutes.

11. Fill pita bowls halfway with rice mixture and tahini sauce.

3.27 Copycat Panera Mediterranean Warm Grain Bowl

Cooking Time: 35 minutes

Serving Size: 2

Ingredients:

- ½ lemon
- ¼ cup tahini dressing
- 1/3 cup feta
- ½ cup Greek yogurt
- ½ cucumber
- ½ cup hummus
- 10 grape tomatoes
- 1/3 cup Kalamata olive
- 2 cups cooked brown rice
- 2 cups arugula
- 2 cups marinade
- 2 chicken breasts

Method:

1. Marinate chicken breasts in Mojo Criollo Marinade overnight.

2. Preheat oven to 350°F and bake for 20 minutes.

3. Follow the package instructions for cooking the rice/quinoa.

4. Place greens along the border of two large serving dishes.

5. Prepare the vegetables.

6. On top of the greens, divide cooked quinoa into two bowls.

7. Mix cucumber, tomatoes, and olives with quinoa/greens.

8. Place the chicken slices on top of the quinoa.

3.28 Mediterranean Quinoa Bowls with Maple Tahini Dressing

Cooking Time: 25 minutes

Serving Size: 4

Ingredients:

For the Quinoa Bowl

- 1 small red onion
- ¼ cup parsley
- 1 English cucumber
- 1-pint cherry tomatoes
- 1 can of black olives
- 1 cup feta cheese
- 2 cups baby spinach
- 1 can artichoke hearts
- 2 cups chicken stock
- 1 cup of quinoa

Maple Tahini Dressing

- 4 tablespoons hot water
- Salt and pepper to taste
- 2 teaspoons maple syrup

- ½ teaspoon oregano
- 1 tablespoon olive oil
- 1 tablespoon red wine vinegar
- Juice of 1 lemon
- ¼ cup tahini

Method:

1. Prepare the quinoa according to the package instructions.

2. Mix the lemon juice, extra virgin olive oil, tahini, maple syrup, red wine vinegar, and oregano to create the dressing.

3. One spoonful at a time, pour in hot water.

4. Whisk until all of the water has been integrated into the dressing.

5. Season with salt and pepper to taste.

Chapter 4: Greek Bowls Recipes

4.1 Skinny Greek Chicken Bowls

Cooking Time: 45 minutes

Serving Size: 4

Ingredients:

Chicken Ingredients

- Salt and pepper
- 2 cups cauliflower rice
- ½ teaspoon basil
- ¾ cup yogurt
- ½ teaspoon oregano
- ½ teaspoon thyme
- 2 tablespoons garlic
- ¼ cup lemon juice
- 2 lbs. chicken tenders

Toppings

- ½ English cucumber
- ½ cup Tzatziki Sauce
- 1 cup tomatoes
- ½ cup red onion
- 2 cups romaine lettuce

Method:

1. Place the diced chicken in a large mixing bowl.

2. Stir in the Greek yogurt, garlic, spices, salt, lemon juice, and pepper until the chopped chicken is well covered.

3. Cook chopped chicken until gently browned on the grill or in the oven.

4. Assemble the bowls: in each of the four bowls, add cooked rice or quinoa.

5. Cooked diced grilled chicken and other fixings go on top.

4.2 Greek Goddess Bulgur Bowls

Cooking Time: 30 minutes

Serving Size: 2

Ingredients:

- Pepper
- 2 teaspoon cooking oil
- ½ cup hummus
- Salt
- 4-ounce grape tomatoes
- 1.5-ounce Greek vinaigrette
- 1-unit red onion
- ½ cup bulgur wheat
- ¼ ounce dill
- ½ cup feta cheese
- 1 tablespoon harissa powder
- 1-unit Persian cucumber
- 13.4-ounce chickpeas

Method:

1. Toss chopped onion and chickpeas on a baking sheet with a big drizzle of oil, harissa powder, and salt.

2. Roast until onion is caramelized and chickpeas are gently browned on the top rack.

3. Meanwhile, mix harissa powder, bulgur, water, and salt in a small saucepan.

4. Bring to a boil, then lower to low heat and cover.

5. Toss half the chopped dill, tomatoes, cucumber, and half the Greek Vinaigrette in a medium mixing bowl.

6. Divide the bulgur among the bowls.

7. Separate the roasted onion and chickpeas and the cucumber feta salad on top.

4.3 Greek Chicken and Potato Bowl

Cooking Time: 6 hours 65 minutes

Serving Size: 4

Ingredients:

- 1 pinch kosher salt
- 1 splash olive oil
- ¼ cup olive oil
- 2 russet potatoes
- 4 cloves garlic
- 1 large lemon
- ¼ teaspoon red pepper flakes
- 1 pinch cayenne pepper
- 1 teaspoon thyme
- 2 teaspoons oregano
- 2 teaspoons black pepper
- 1 teaspoon rosemary
- 2 teaspoons kosher salt
- 2 pounds chicken thighs

For the Salad

- 1 cup feta cheese
- 4 cups salad greens
- 2 cups cherry tomatoes
- ½ cup red onion
- 2 cups English cucumber

For the Dressing

- 2 tablespoons parsley
- 2 tablespoons oregano
- 1 large lemon
- Salt and black pepper
- ⅓ cup olive oil
- ¼ cup red wine vinegar

Method:

1. Combine the oregano, chicken thighs, rosemary, sea salt, pepper, thyme, cayenne, garlic, lemon juice, red pepper flakes, and olive oil in a large mixing bowl.

2. Preheat oven to 475 degrees Fahrenheit.

3. Place the chicken thighs on the sheet pan.

4. Roast until the meat is cooked through in the middle of a preheated oven.

5. While the meat and potatoes are heating, make the dressing by whisking together salt, olive oil, lemon juice, red wine vinegar, and pepper.

6. Remove the potatoes with a spatula after allowing them to cool for a few minutes.

4.4 Greek Chicken Salad Lunch Bowls

Cooking Time: 15 minutes

Serving Size: 5

Ingredients:

For the Bowls

- 1 large cucumber
- 1 cup cherry tomatoes
- ½ cup feta
- ⅔ cup kalamata olives
- 1 cup hummus
- 1 cup tzatziki
- 4 cups chicken
- 6 cups baby spinach

For the Greek Dressing

- Pinch of fine sea salt
- ¼ teaspoon black pepper
- 1 ½ teaspoons oregano
- 1 teaspoon garlic powder
- ½ cup olive oil
- 1 ½ teaspoons basil
- 2 tablespoons red wine vinegar
- 3 tablespoons lemon juice

Method:

1. In a mason jar, combine all of the ingredients to create the dressing.

2. Fill five lunch containers halfway with mixed greens, then equally distribute the tzatziki, hummus, feta, chicken, cucumber, olives, and tomatoes.

3. Refrigerate for up to five days before serving.

4.5 Instant Pot Greek Chicken Rice Bowl

Cooking Time:

Serving Size: 4

Ingredients:

For the Chicken Bowl

- 1 cup chicken breast
- 1 teaspoon lemon pepper
- ¼ teaspoon salt
- 1/8 teaspoon black pepper
- 1 teaspoon oregano
- 1 teaspoon garlic
- 1 cup chicken broth
- ½ cup white rice
- 1 tablespoon butter
- Juice and zest lemon
- 1 tablespoon olive oil

For the Tzatziki Sauce

- 1/8 teaspoon garlic
- 1 teaspoon olive oil
- 1/16 teaspoon black pepper
- ¼ teaspoon dill

- 1 teaspoon lemon juice
- 1/8 teaspoon salt
- 3 tablespoon cucumber
- 4 ½ tablespoon yogurt

For the Topping

- 2 tablespoons red onion
- 2 tablespoon cucumber
- 2 tablespoons red bell pepper
- 2 tablespoon feta cheese
- 2 tablespoon Kalamata olives
- 2 tablespoon tomato

Method:

1. Combine all sauces ingredients in a bowl dish or jar and chill until ready to use.

2. Add lemon juice butter, oil, and zest, broth, salt, oregano, rice, garlic, and black pepper to create the Chicken Bowl.

3. Toss the chicken with the lemon pepper in a small dish, then distribute it equally over the rice.

4. Fill a serving dish halfway with chicken and rice, then top with bell pepper, onion, feta, cucumber, tomatoes, and olives.

5. Serve with tzatziki sauce right away.

4.6 Marinated Greek Chickpea Bowls

Cooking Time: 25 minutes

Serving Size: 2

Ingredients:

Marinated Chickpeas

- ¼ teaspoon salt
- A pinch of black pepper
- ½ cup red peppers
- 1 teaspoon oregano
- ½ small lemon
- 3 cloves garlic
- ¼ cup olive oil
- ¼ fresh parsley
- ¼ cup red wine vinegar
- 1 15 oz. can chickpeas

Bowl Toppings

- Fresh lemon
- White rice
- Homemade tzatziki sauce
- Garlic herb pita chips
- ½ cup feta cheese
- 1 cup cherry tomatoes
- ½ English cucumber

Method:

1. Fill a bowl halfway with chickpeas.

2. Squeeze the lemon and add the parsley, fresh garlic, and roasted red peppers.

3. Combine the olive oil, red wine vinegar, and spices in a mixing bowl.

4. Season to taste and season with salt if necessary.

5. Assemble the bowl after everything is finished!

4.7 Greek Lentil Power Bowl

Cooking Time: 40 minutes

Serving Size: 3

Ingredients:

- ¼ cup feta
- Salt and pepper to taste
- ¼ cup red onion
- ½ cup chickpeas
- ½ cup cucumber
- ½ cup cherry tomatoes
- 1 tablespoon lemon juice
- 1 teaspoon honey
- 1 cup brown lentils
- ¼ cup Greek yogurt
- 1 tablespoon dill
- 2 cup water

Method:

1. In a saucepan, combine the water, lentils, and salt and bring to a boil.

2. Cover and lower the heat to low after the water has reached a boil.

3. Cook for 35-minutes, or until all of the water has been absorbed.

4. Mix the dill, lemon juice, Greek yogurt, and honey in a separate dish while the lentils are cooking.

5. Set aside after stirring with a spoon.

6. Serve with a Greek yogurt dressing on the side.

4.8 Greek Bowl with Salmon

Cooking Time: 42 minutes

Serving Size: 4

Ingredients:

Bowl

- ½ cup feta cheese
- 1 avocado
- 1 can garbanzo beans
- ⅓ cup kalamata olives
- 1 cup tomatoes
- ½ cup red onion
- 4 cups romaine
- 1 cup English cucumber
- 1 ½ cups cooked quinoa
- 4 salmon fillets

Marinade

- ½ teaspoon sea salt
- ¼ teaspoon black pepper
- 2 cloves garlic

- 1 teaspoon honey
- 2 tablespoon oregano leaves
- 1 tablespoon fresh dill
- 1 lemon
- ½ cup olive oil

Tzatziki

- ¼ teaspoon sea salt
- ¼ teaspoon black pepper
- 1 tablespoon fresh dill
- 2 cloves garlic
- 1 ½ tablespoon lemon juice
- 1 tablespoon olive oil
- ½ cup Greek yogurt
- ½ cup English cucumber

Method:

1. Preheat the oven to 450 degrees Fahrenheit.
2. Mix the marinade ingredients in a bowl.
3. In a shallow dish, place the salmon.
4. Pour half of the mixture over the salmon and left to marinate for fifteen minutes.
5. Bake for 9-12 minutes in a preheated oven.
6. Combine the cherry tomatoes, red onion, cucumber slices, and garbanzo beans in a mixing dish.
7. Toss in the rest of the marinade.
8. In a mixing bowl, add all of the Tzatziki sauce components and stir gently to incorporate.

9. Make a set of four or five bowls.

Chapter 5: Lebanese Bowls Recipes

5.1 Lebanese Buddha Bowl with Tahini Drizzle

Cooking Time: 30 minutes

Serving Size: 4

Ingredients:

For the Beetroot Couscous

- 2 tablespoons fresh lemon juice
- Black Pepper, to taste
- 2 small cooked beetroot
- 1 teaspoon bouillon powder
- 240ml water
- 100g couscous

For the Falafel

- Black pepper
- Sesame seeds
- 1 coriander
- 2 tablespoon aquafaba
- 4 tablespoon breadcrumbs
- 1 parsley
- 1 tablespoon cumin
- 1 tablespoon tahini
- 400g tin chickpeas
- 1 small onion

- 2 cloves garlic

For the Tahini Dressing

- A little water

- Black pepper

- 1 cloves garlic

- 1 lemon

- 4 tablespoon tahini

Method:

1. Place the large grains, beetroot, water, and bouillon in a pan and simmer gently for the couscous.

2. Cook for a further 8 minutes.

3. Set aside to cool after seasoning with lemon and black pepper.

4. Preheat the oven to 180 degrees Celsius.

5. Pulse all of the components for the falafel in a food processor, except the sesame seeds.

6. With moist hands, form golf ball-sized portions of the falafel paste into balls or patties.

7. Preheat the oven to 350°F and bake for half an hour.

8. Place a couple of pieces of falafel on top of some of the couscous.

5.2 Lebanese Falafel Bowls

Cooking Time: 24 minutes

Serving Size: 4

Ingredients:

- Zesty tahini dressing
- Pita bread
- ¼ cup feta
- ¼ cup onions
- ½ cup tzatziki
- ¼ cup harissa
- 2 cups Israeli salad
- ½ cup hummus
- 1 cup purple cabbage
- 1 batch falafel
- 2 cups brown rice
- 4 cups baby spinach

Method:

1. Prepare all falafel, Israeli salad, hummus, tzatziki, and tahini dressing ahead of time.

2. Toss white rice, baby spinach, and purple cabbage into separate dishes.

3. Mix 3-4 cooked harissa, falafel patties, tzatziki, feta, Israeli salad, hummus, and pickled onions into each bowl.

5.3 Lebanese Vegetarian Bowl

Cooking Time: 30 minutes

Serving Size: 4

Ingredients:

Tahini Rice Salad

- 1 spring onion
- 40g pomegranate seeds
- 1 teaspoon tamari
- 2 tablespoons plain yogurt
- 2 teaspoon tahini
- 100g brown rice

Spiced Chickpeas

- 4 radishes
- 2 lemon wedges
- 2 red peppers hummus
- 1 avocado
- 2 handfuls salad leaves
- 10 large green olives
- 1 teaspoon cumin
- 1 teaspoon paprika
- Pinch salt
- 0.5 teaspoon turmeric
- 1 tablespoon olive oil
- 1 x 400g tin chickpeas

Method:

1. Cook the brown rice according to the package directions.

2. Mix in the pomegranate seeds and finely chopped spring onion, then put aside.

3. To prepare the spiced chickpeas, drain the canned chickpeas and combine with the paprika, salt, cumin, olive oil, and turmeric in a medium saucepan.

4. Cook for five minutes over medium-high heat!

5. Build the two buddha bowls at this point.

5.4 Lebanese Bean Salad Bowl

Cooking Time: 23 minutes

Serving Size: 4

Ingredients:

Lebanese Bean Salad Bowls

- 1 can bean salad
- ½ cup prepared hummus
- 1/8 teaspoon salt and pepper
- ¼ cup fresh parsley
- 1 cup couscous
- 1 cup vegetable broth
- ¼ cup shallots
- 1 tablespoon olive oil

Lemon Parsley Dressing

- ½ teaspoon Dijon mustard
- ¼ cup olive oil

- ½ teaspoon salt

- ¼ teaspoon pepper

- 1 large lemon

- 1 small garlic clove

- ½ cup parsley

Method:

1. Add oil to a small saucepan and heat over medium-high heat.

2. Add the shallots and cook for another 2-3 minutes.

3. Sauté for a further minute, or until the couscous is gently toasted.

4. Bring the stock and salt to a boil, then remove from the heat.

5. In a small bowl, whisk the lemon juice/zest, pepper, parsley, salt, garlic, and mustard until the mustard is incorporated.

6. Season with salt and pepper to taste, if required.

7. Stir the dressing into the couscous.

8. Prepare the bowls.

5.5 Lebanese Cauliflower Bowls

Cooking Time: 1 hour

Serving Size: 4

Ingredients:

For the Baba Ganoush

- 1 teaspoon ground cumin
- Juice 1 lemon
- 1 ½ tablespoon tahini
- ½ chili powder
- ½ tablespoon olive oil
- 2 garlic cloves
- 2 large aubergines

For the Cauliflower

- ½ olive oil
- Juice ½ lemon
- 1 ½ tablespoon shawarma spice mix
- 600g cauliflower florets

For the Tabbouleh

- 2 spring onions
- 50g pomegranate seeds
- 3 tomatoes
- 1 cucumber
- Large handful parsley
- Small handful mint

- 3 tablespoons olive oil

- Juice 1 ½ lemons

- 400g tin chickpeas

- 100g bulgur wheat

Method:

1. Preheat the oven to 200 degrees Celsius.

2. Toss the spice mix, cauliflower, and lots of seasoning in a large roasting pan.

3. Drizzle the olive oil over the top and roast for 30 minutes, or until the vegetables are just soft.

4. Set aside the lemon juice that has been squeezed over it.

5. In the meanwhile, prepare the baba ganoush.

6. Season with salt and pepper to taste, then put aside.

7. Bring the bulgur wheat and water to a boil in a medium saucepan.

8. Simmer for 8-10 minutes, covered.

9. Stir in the remaining tabbouleh ingredients, as well as a generous amount of spice.

5.6 Lebanese Ground Beef Bowl

Cooking Time: 20 minutes

Serving Size: 6

Ingredients:

- ½ teaspoon mint leaves
- ¼ teaspoon ginger
- 1 teaspoon allspice
- ½ teaspoon cayenne pepper
- 2 teaspoons cumin
- 1 ½ teaspoons cinnamon
- ¼ cup water
- 2 tablespoons coriander
- 1 ½ teaspoon Kosher salt
- ½ teaspoon black pepper
- 1 large yellow onion
- 4 cloves garlic
- 2 pounds beef

Method:

1. Combine the onion, ground beef, salt, and pepper in a large pan over medium-high heat.

2. Cook the meat until it is browned, breaking it up as you go.

3. Stir the water, cayenne, cumin, mint leaves, cinnamon, coriander, allspice, and ginger together in a small cup.

4. Remove any extra fat before adding the spices.

5. Cook, constantly stirring, until the water has evaporated.

5.7 Lebanese Bowl with Tahini Yogurt Sauce

Cooking Time: 8 hours 40 minutes

Serving Size: 6

Ingredients:

Tahini Yogurt Sauce

- Salt and pepper to taste
- ½ cup water
- 1 garlic clove
- ½ lemon
- ½ cup Yogurt
- ½ cup tahini paste

Falafel

- ½ teaspoon baking powder
- Vegetable grapeseed oil
- 3 tablespoons flour
- 1 teaspoon baking soda
- ½ teaspoon cayenne
- 2 teaspoon cumin
- 2 teaspoons kosher salt
- 1 tablespoon coriander
- 1 bunch parsley
- 1 bunch cilantro
- 1 yellow onion

- 4 garlic cloves
- 2 cups chickpeas

Falafel Bowl

- Homemade hummus
- Olive oil
- Dried oregano
- Zaatar
- Cubed feta
- Salad greens Arugula

Israeli Chopped Salad

- 1-2 tablespoons lemon juice
- Olive oil
- 1 teaspoon dried mint
- ½ teaspoon Kosher salt
- 2 tomatoes
- 2 Persian cucumbers

Method:

1. Soak the dry chickpeas in a big bowl of water.

2. Drain chickpeas and pulse until finely crushed in a food processor, then transfer to a large mixing bowl and set aside.

3. Pulse the onion, herbs, garlic, and spices in the same food processor until finely ground, then add the combination of the herbs to the crushed chickpeas.

4. Combine the baking soda, flour, and baking powder in a mixing bowl.

5. Meanwhile, heat the vegetable oil in a big pan.

6. Fry 4-6 falafel till golden brown on both sides, about 3-5 minutes on each side.

7. In a small food processor, combine all of the ingredients for the tahini yogurt sauce and pulse until smooth.

5.8 Braised Lebanese Lentil Freekeh Bowl

Cooking Time: 35 minutes

Serving Size: 10

Ingredients:

- 1 teaspoon pepper
- 20 oz. black forest ham
- ¼ cup lemon juice
- 2 teaspoon cayenne
- 4 cups kale
- 3 tablespoon canola oil
- 1/3 cup pine nuts
- 1 cup red bell peppers
- ½ cup currants
- 2 quarts of beef stock
- 2 cups freekeh
- 1 tablespoon cinnamon
- 2 ½ cups lentils

Method:

1. Combine cinnamon, lentils, currants, freekeh, and stock in a slow cooker.

2. Cook for 35 minutes on high.

3. Combine pine nuts, oil, kale, lemon juice, cayenne pepper, red pepper, and pepper in a mixing bowl.

4. Allow the greens to soften and wilt gently.

5. Serve in dishes with chopped ham on top of each serving.

Chapter 6: Vegetarian Bowls Recipes

6.1 Ratatouille Bowl with Buckwheat and Burrata

Cooking Time: 1 hour

Serving Size: 6

Ingredients:

For the French Ratatouille

- 4 thyme sprigs
- Salt and black pepper
- 5 large tomatoes
- 1 tablespoon tomato paste
- 1 yellow onion
- 5 garlic cloves
- 2 zucchinis
- 3 bell peppers
- Extra virgin olive oil
- 1 large eggplant

Other Ingredients

- A pinch of salt
- 2 fresh burrata balls
- 3,5 cups water
- 2 cups buckwheat

Method:

1. In a large nonstick skillet, heat approximately three tablespoons of olive oil over moderate flame.

2. Separately cook the zucchini, eggplants, and bell peppers until tender and beginning to brown.

3. Toss in another tablespoon of oil, followed by the onion and tomato paste.

4. Heat for about 5 minutes.

5. Cook for 10 - 15 minutes after adding the cooked zucchini, eggplant, and bell peppers to the pan.

6. In a kettle or saucepan, bring 3 cups of water to a boil with a pinch of salt.

7. Two cups buckwheat stirred in and brought back to a boil.

8. In each serving dish, divide the buckwheat, then top with the ratatouille.

6.2 Spring Abundance Bowl

Cooking Time: 40 minutes

Serving Size: 4

Ingredients:

Meyer Lemon and Shallot Dressing

- 1 teaspoon Dijon mustard
- 4 tablespoons olive oil
- 1 ½ tablespoon Meyer lemon juice
- ½ teaspoon salt
- 1 Meyer lemon
- 1 shallot

For the Bowl

- 1 small beet
- 1 tablespoon hemp seeds

- 1 ripe avocado
- 1 cup pea shoots
- 1 small bay leaf
- 4 ounces goat cheese
- 1 cup lentils
- 1 clove garlic
- ½ teaspoon salt
- 1 cup quinoa

Method:

1. In a jar, combine all of the ingredients.

2. Over medium-high heat, combine water, quinoa, and salt in a small saucepan.

3. Bring to a boil, then reduce to low heat.

4. In a small pot, place the lentils.

5. Fill the container with two inches of water.

6. In a separate bowl, combine the garlic and bay leaf.

7. Over moderate heat, cook for 20-25 minutes.

8. Remove the bay leaf and garlic cloves with a slotted spoon, drain, and put aside.

9. In four bowls, divide the heated quinoa and lentils.

6.3 Ancient Grain Bowls with Pistachio Cashew Cheese

Cooking Time: 30 minutes

Serving Size: 2

Ingredients:

- 4 oz. baby arugula
- 1 tablespoon olive oil
- 1 lemon
- 1 apple
- 2 tablespoon pistachios
- 2 oz. cashew cheese
- 2 tablespoon vegan butter
- 2 oz. sliced leeks
- 1 tablespoon mustard & herb blend

Method:

1. Preheat oven to 425 degrees Fahrenheit.
2. In a medium saucepan over high heat, combine water, barley, and a pinch of salt.
3. Bring to a boil, then reduce to low heat for 25 minutes.
4. On a baking sheet, mix French mustard & herb blend, olive oil, chickpeas, and a sprinkle of salt. 10 - 15 minutes, or until caramelized and crispy in parts.
5. In a large nonstick skillet, melt butter over low heat.
6. Add the leeks and season with salt and pepper.

7. Finely chop pistachios and sprinkle with salt and pepper.

8. In a medium mixing bowl, combine the lemon juice, sliced apple, arugula, olive oil, and a sprinkle of salt and pepper.

9. Toss the arugula and apple salad together.

6.4 Lentil Salad Bowl with Sweet Peppers and Basil

Cooking Time: 30 minutes

Serving Size: 4

Ingredients:

Salad

- 1 large avocado
- ½ cup fresh basil
- ⅔ cup sweet onion
- 1 sweet bell pepper
- 4 cups green lentils

Dressing

- 1 teaspoon chili powder
- ½ teaspoon sea salt
- 2 tablespoons lemon juice
- 2 tablespoons olive oil

Method:

1. In a large mixing bowl, add all of the salad components and gently toss to incorporate.

2. In a small mixing bowl, whisk together all of the dressing ingredients.

3. Toss the salad with the dressing and toss lightly to incorporate.

4. Fill bowls with the mixture and serve at room temperature, or cover and chill for two or more hours to serve cold.

6.5 Farro Bowl with Kale & Figs

Cooking Time: 20 minutes

Serving Size: 2

Ingredients:

- 2 tablespoons walnuts
- 2 ounces goat cheese
- 2 large handfuls of kale
- 4 figs
- 1 ½ cups cooked farro

Balsamic Maple Mustard Dressing

- ½ teaspoon kosher salt
- ¼ teaspoon pepper
- 2 teaspoons maple syrup
- 1 teaspoon mustard
- 2 tablespoons balsamic
- 2 tablespoons olive oil

Method:

1. In a small mixing bowl, combine the dressing ingredients.

2. Divide farro between two bowls.

3. Massage kale in a mixing bowl with a sprinkle of salt and a drizzle of olive oil until it is covered and malleable.

4. Divide the kale amongst the dishes.

5. Add the figs and goat cheese over the top.

6.6 Instant Pot Burrito Bowls with Black Beans and Brown Rice

Cooking Time: 1 hour 10 minutes

Serving Size: 4

Ingredients:

Corn Salsa

- 2 tablespoons cilantro
- ½ jalapeno
- juice of 1 lime
- 2 tablespoons red onion
- 2 ears corn

Brown Rice

- Juice of ½ lime
- 1/8 cup cilantro
- ½ teaspoon sea salt
- 1 bay leaf
- 1 cup water
- 1 cup brown rice

Black Beans

- ¼ teaspoon sea salt
- Juice of 1 lime

- 1 tablespoon oregano
- 1 tablespoon cumin
- 4 cups water
- 1 bay leaf
- 3 cloves garlic
- 2 cups black beans
- 1 yellow onion
- 1 teaspoon olive oil

Other Toppings

- 1 cup guacamole
- 1 cup salsa
- 1 heart Romaine lettuce

Method:

1. In an Instant Pot, heat the oil, if using, on sauté mode.

2. Add the onion and cook until it is soft.

3. Combine the bay leaf, oregano, water, cumin, beans, and salt in a large mixing bowl.

4. Combine the salt, water, rice, and bay leaf in a mixing bowl.

5. Place the rice dish on top of the beans on a trivet.

6. While the beans cook, the rice will steam.

7. Squeeze lime juice over the rice and beans.

8. Season with salt and pepper to taste.

6.7 Acai Bowls

Cooking Time: 5 minutes

Serving Size: 2

Ingredients:

- ¼ cup banana
- 2 sprigs mint
- ¼ cup granola
- ¼ cup fresh berries
- 1 cup frozen fruit
- 1 banana
- 7 ounces frozen acai

Method:

1. While the frozen acai is still in the package, break it up into big pieces.

2. Remove the frozen fruit, frozen acai pieces, and banana from the package and put them in a food processor.

3. Alternatively, mix the ingredients in a blender with a little juice.

4. Sprinkle granola and fresh fruit over the combined mixture in a dish or bowls.

6.8 Pitaya Bowl

Cooking Time: 7 minutes

Serving Size: 1

Ingredients:

- Kiwi chunks
- Coconut shreds
- Berries
- Banana slices
- Hemp seeds
- Granola
- 1/3 cup coconut water
- Chia seeds
- 1 pack frozen Pitaya

Method:

1. Break up the frozen pitaya into pieces using your hands.

2. Blend in any additional frozen fruit and a little amount of liquid.

3. Blend until everything is thoroughly blended.

4. Fill a bowl halfway with the frozen mixture and top with your preferred toppings.

6.9 Quinoa Taco Bowls

Cooking Time: 20 minutes

Serving Size: 4

Ingredients:

Quinoa Taco Bowls

- Tortilla Chips
- Tortillas
- Quick Guacamole
- Store-Bought Salsa
- 3 Roma tomatoes
- 1 cilantro
- 1 can of pinto beans
- 1 romaine lettuce
- 1 can of black beans
- 2 cups cooked quinoa

Easy Guacamole

- Juice of 1 lime
- Garlic salt to taste
- 2 large ripe avocados

Method:

1. In a large skillet, heat the olive oil over medium heat.

2. Add the beans and cook until they are heated.

3. Taco spice may be added to taste.

4. Set the table with quinoa, tomatoes, lettuce, cilantro, seasoned beans, salsa, cheese, guacamole, and chips or tortillas.

5. In a small bowl, mash the avocados with lime juice.

6. Toss in a pinch of garlic salt to taste.

6.10 Chili-Orange Veggie Bowl

Cooking Time: 1 hour

Serving Size: 2

Ingredients:

- Extra-virgin olive oil
- Sea salt & pepper
- Handful of sprouts
- Sprinkle of sesame seeds
- A few slabs of tofu
- ¼ cup pomegranate seeds
- 1 bunch of broccolini
- 2 small carrots
- 1 sweet potato
- A few scallions
- ½ cup rice

Chili-Orange Vinaigrette

- 1 teaspoon chili paste
- 1 teaspoon rice vinegar
- 1 teaspoon soy sauce
- 1 teaspoon sesame oil

- 2 tablespoons orange juice

Method:

1. Cook the rice according to the rice cooker's directions.

2. Make sure you use a shallow skillet.

3. In separate steamer trays, place the sweet potatoes and broccolini.

4. Add the scallions and a touch of salt and pepper on top.

5. Afterward, make the dressing and put it aside.

6. Toss carrot ribbons with a sprinkle of salt and a splash of rice vinegar.

7. Allow marinating in the refrigerator until ready to use.

8. In a skillet, heat the oil, then add the tofu and continue cooking on each side.

6.11 Roasted Veggie Winter Bliss Bowl

Cooking Time: 30 minutes

Serving Size: 2

Ingredients:

- Olive oil
- Salt and black pepper
- ¼ red onion
- Handful of mushrooms
- 1 cup butternut squash
- A handful of green beans
- ½ yellow bell pepper
- 10 cherry tomatoes
- 1 cup Brussels sprouts
- 2 small beets
- 1 cup French lentils
- 2 cups red quinoa

Tahini Dressing

- Water
- Juice of ½ lemon
- ¼ cup tahini

Method:

1. Preheat the oven to 375 degrees Fahrenheit.

2. Season the veggies with salt and pepper after tossing them in a large quantity of olive oil.

3. Place on a baking sheet in a single layer and roast for 20-half an hour.

4. With enough water, thin the tahini and lemon to a dripping consistency.

5. In two dishes, divide the heated quinoa and lentils.

6. Add the roasted veggies on top.

6.12 Vegetarian Chili Bowl

Cooking Time: 30 minutes

Serving Size: 4

Ingredients:

For the Pickled Onions

- Large pinch of kosher salt
- Small pinch of sugar
- 1 red onion
- 1 lime

For the Chili

- Kosher salt
- Fresh cilantro
- 2 cans beans
- 1 (15-ounce) can of tomatoes
- 1 teaspoon chili powder
- 1 teaspoon oregano
- 1 large onion
- 3 garlic cloves
- Olive oil

Method:

1. In a mixing dish, pour the lime juice and add onion, salt, and sugar.

2. In a large skillet, heat the oil over medium-high heat. Pour in the oil.

3. When the pan is heated, add the onion and cook for approximately five minutes or softened.

4. Sauté for 1 to 2 minutes longer, until chili powder, garlic, and oregano are aromatic.

5. Add the beans and tomatoes, as well as a couple of big pinches of salt, and cook until the tomatoes have broken down.

6. Taste and season with more chili powder, salt, and oregano as desired.

6.13 Lentil Bowls with Fried Eggs & Greens

Cooking Time: 40 minutes

Serving Size: 4

Ingredients:

- 2 teaspoons olive oil
- 4 large eggs
- 12 green olives
- 1 avocado
- 4 cups baby spinach
- 1 cup red peppers
- ¼ teaspoon pepper
- 8 cups kale
- 1 tablespoon lemon juice
- ½ teaspoon salt
- ¼ cup Greek yogurt
- 1 teaspoon lemon zest
- 2 ½ cups water
- 2 cloves garlic
- 1 bay leaf
- ½ cup green lentils

Method:

1. In a medium saucepan over high heat, bring water to a boil.

2. Stir in the crushed garlic, lentils, and bay leaf.

3. Cook for 25 to 30 minutes, or until the lentils are cooked.

4. Add pepper, yogurt, salt, lemon juice, lemon zest, and chopped garlic in a large mixing bowl.

5. Toss in the greens and spinach to coat.

6. Serve the kale mixture in 4 dinner dishes with roasted red peppers on top.

7. In a large nonstick skillet, heat the oil over medium-high heat.

8. Crack the eggs into the pan one at a time.

9. Serve with an egg on top of each bowl.

6.14 Italian Vegetable Rice Bowl

Cooking Time: 25 minutes

Serving Size: 1

Ingredients:

- Olive oil
- 2 tablespoons wine vinegar
- Salt and peppers
- Parsley
- 1 cup parmesan
- 1 ½ ounces parmesan
- Eight small artichoke
- 2 tablespoons lemon juice
- 1 tablespoon butter
- 6 cups vegetable stock
- 1 shallot
- 1 clove garlic
- 1 ⅔ cups risotto

Method:

1. In a pan, heat the olive oil and cook the shallots and rice until transparent.

2. Stir in the garlic and stock gently.

3. Cut the artichokes in the meanwhile.

4. Cook in lots of boiling water for approximately 7 minutes.

5. Stir the parmesan cheese into the risotto just before serving and season with salt & pepper to taste.

6. In a deep fryer, heat the oil and gently cook the artichokes.

7. Reduce the heat and season with salt and pepper to taste.

6.15 Grilled Veggie bowl

Cooking Time: 35 minutes

Serving Size: 4

Ingredients:

Lemon Dressing

- 1 teaspoon oregano
- Kosher salt and black pepper
- ½ teaspoon Dijon mustard
- 2 cloves garlic
- 1/3 cup red wine vinegar
- 2 tablespoons lemon juice
- ½ cup olive oil

Grilled Vegetables

- Olive oil
- Salt and black pepper
- 2 medium bell peppers
- 8 ounces mushrooms
- 2 medium zucchinis
- 1 red onion

Bowls

- Salt and black pepper
- Pita chips or pita bread
- ½ cup feta cheese
- Fresh dill and basil

- 1 cup grape tomatoes

- ½ cup Kalamata olives

- 15 oz. chickpeas

- 1 cucumber

- 2 cups cooked farro

Method:

1. Heat the grill to a high setting.

2. Season the veggies with salt and pepper after drizzling them with olive oil.

3. Grill the vegetables.

4. Stir together the red wine vinegar, olive oil, salt, Dijon mustard, oregano, lemon juice, garlic, and black pepper to make the dressing.

5. Roughly cut the grilled veggies before assembling the bowls.

6. Divide the farro among four bowls and top with the steamed veggies in each.

6.16 Veggie Nourish Bowl

Cooking Time: 1 hour

Serving Size: 4

Ingredients:

- 2 small cucumbers
- 2 avocados
- 1 cup canned corn
- 1 cup black beans
- 1 acorn squash
- 2 bunches of baby broccoli
- 2 teaspoons sesame oil
- 1 teaspoon miso
- 1 teaspoon cumin
- ½ teaspoon curry powder
- Black pepper
- 1 head cauliflower
- ½ teaspoon onion powder
- Kosher salt
- 1 teaspoon paprika
- 1 teaspoon garlic powder
- 4 potatoes
- 1 teaspoon Italian herb seasoning
- 3 tablespoons olive oil

Method:

1. Preheat the oven to 400 degrees Fahrenheit.

2. Toss potatoes with spices.

3. Toss cauliflower with spices.

4. Toss in with the potatoes in the pan.

5. Combine sesame oil and miso in a bowl.

6. Roast the cauliflower for half an hour or until golden brown.

7. Bring a saucepan of water to a boil in the meanwhile.

8. Three minutes to blanch the young broccoli.

9. Over a moderate flame, heat a dry skillet.

10. For a few minutes, sear the corn kernels.

11. To serve, combine all ingredients in two dishes.

6.17 Brilliantly Balanced Veggie Burrito Bowl

Cooking Time: 30 minutes

Serving Size: 4

Ingredients:

- 1 spring onion
- 1 lime
- 5.5g vegetable stock mix
- 125g cherry tomatoes
- 5g coriander
- 100g brown rice
- 1 natural yogurt
- 1 chipotle paste sachet
- 1 red pepper
- 2 teaspoons smoked paprika
- 1 tomato paste sachet
- 1 yellow pepper
- 1 can of black beans
- 1 red onion

Method:

1. Preheat the oven to 220 degrees Celsius.

2. In a baking pan, combine the peppers and red onion wedges.

3. With a drizzle of olive oil, add the smoked paprika.

4. Preheat the oven to 200°F and bake the tray for 20-25 minutes.

5. In a small dish, combine the cherry tomatoes and spring.

6. In a small bowl, mix the lime zest, natural yogurt, and lime juice.

7. Heat a wide-bottomed pan over medium heat with a sprinkle of olive oil.

8. Add the drained black beans, tomato paste, and chipotle paste once the pan is heated.

9. Cook for 5-6 minutes after adding the veggie stock.

10. Add a dollop of lime yogurt on top.

6.18 Calabrian Bean & Veggie Bowls

Cooking Time: 35 minutes

Serving Size: 2

Ingredients:

- 2 tablespoons olive oil
- Salt and pepper
- 2 tablespoon white sesame seeds
- 5.3 oz. chili pepper beans
- 1 lime
- ½ oz. fresh basil
- 6 oz. parsnip
- 4 oz. roasted red peppers
- 3 garlic cloves
- 6 oz. broccolini
- ⅓ cup cashews
- ¾ cup farro

Method:

1. Preheat the oven to 375 degrees Fahrenheit.

2. In a small saucepan, combine farro and a pinch of salt.

3. Bring to a boil, lower to medium, and simmer for 18 to 20 minutes, or until farro is soft.

4. Toss broccolini with olive oil and a sprinkle of salt and pepper.

5. 12 to 15 minutes, or until soft and browned in spots.

6. To make the basil cashew sauce, combine all ingredients in a blender and blend until smooth.

7. Cook, three to five minutes, until cooked farro grains are glossy and toasted.

8. Season to taste with salt and pepper.

9. Divide toasted farro into big bowls.

6.19 Vegetarian Banh Mi Bowls

Cooking Time: 40 minutes

Serving Size: 4

Ingredients:

- ½ cup peanuts
- ½ cup cilantro
- ½ cup mayonnaise
- 2 tablespoons sriracha sauce
- 1 tablespoon sesame oil
- 1 teaspoon salt
- ¼ cup water
- ¼ cup white sugar
- 6 radishes
- ½ cup rice vinegar
- 1 cucumber
- 2 carrots
- 1-quart water
- ¼ package quinoa
- ½ package brown rice
- 3 quarts water

Method:

1. Fill a bowl halfway with cooked quinoa.

2. In a mixing bowl, combine the carrots, cucumber, and radishes.

3. In a small saucepan, bring the vinegar, sesame oil, sugar, water, and salt to a boil.

4. Pour the mixture over the veggies in the bowl.

5. Allow sitting for 20 minutes before draining.

6. In a small bowl, mix mayonnaise and sriracha sauce while the veggies are pickling.

6.20 Spanish Rice Bowl with Taco Spice

Cooking Time: 25 minutes

Serving Size: 1

Ingredients:

- Salt
- Potato flour
- Lemon juice
- Spices
- Garlic
- Parsley
- Crushed tomatoes
- Raisins
- Olive Oil
- Almonds
- Kalamata olives
- Water
- Buckwheat
- Brown rice
- Feta
- Red peppers
- Chickpeas
- Yellow peppers
- Kale
- Onion

Method:

1. In a nonstick saucepan over medium heat, mix one teaspoon neutral oil and one tablespoon water.
2. Cover and cook for 10 to 15 minutes, or until internal temperature has reached 165° F.

Conclusion

Mediterranean cuisine includes fresh grains, meats, veggies, and olives. Mediterranean meals are popular among people all over the globe because of the many nutritional advantages they offer. As it promotes fresh, low-fat, lipid-free foods, the Mediterranean diet is heart-healthy. This implies that you should try this dish whether you're trying to lose weight or just don't enjoy eating unhealthy meals. While this diet contains some animal protein, it is in tiny quantities and is low in fat, both of which are good for your health. Mediterranean cuisine is renowned for its delicious tastes and health advantages all over the globe. This diet has the benefit of enabling you to eat healthy, whole foods. Because the diet consists mostly of fruits, nuts, and vegetables, you don't have to be conscious about your diet. Make healthier meals for your family by preparing side meals with Mediterranean bowls cuisine.